I Love My Dachshund

Abigail Beal

PowerKiDS press
New York

This book is dedicated to you and your pet— a special friendship based on loyalty, respect, and kindness.

Published in 2011 by The Rosen Publishing Group, Inc.
29 East 21st Street, New York, NY 10010

First Edition

Editor: Joanne Randolph
Book Design: Greg Tucker

Photo Credits: Cover, pp. 4, 8–9, 10 (left). 10–11, 11 (right), 13, 18 (left), 18–19, 19 (right), 20 (left),20– 21, 22 Shutterstock.com; p. 5 Manzo Niikura/Getty Images; p. 6 Sasha/Stringer/Getty Images; p. 7 H. D. Barlow/Getty Images; p. 12 © H Schmidt-Roeger/age fotostock; p. 14 Comstock/Thinkstock; p. 15 JGI/Tom Grill/Getty Images; p. 16 Brand X Pictures/Thinkstock; p. 17 Hemera/Thinkstock.

Library of Congress Cataloging-in-Publication Data

Beal, Abigail.
 I love my dachshund / by Abigail Beal. — 1st ed.
    p. cm. — (Top dogs)
 Includes index.
 ISBN 978-1-4488-2537-0 (library binding) — ISBN 978-1-4488-2658-2 (pbk.) —
ISBN 978-1-4488-2659-9 (6-pack)
 1. Dachshunds—Juvenile literature. I. Title.
 SF429.D25B43 2011
 636.753'8—dc22
                              2010025264

Manufactured in the United States of America

CPSIA Compliance Information: Batch #WW11PK: For Further Information contact Rosen Publishing, New York, New York at 1-800-237-9932

Contents

Meet the Dachshund

The dachshund is a well-liked **domestic** family pet. Because of its long shape, this **breed** is often called the hot dog or wiener dog. Many dachshund owners also call this breed the doxie. Doxies are full of **personality** and **charm**. Whether you are playing a game of fetch or teaching your

Dachshunds are long and low to the ground. Their long bodies and short legs are what lead people to call them hot dogs!

pet **obedience** skills, you will find that the dachshund is happy to be with you.

People like dachshunds because they are **social**. This is a dog that likes to be with its people. Are you ready to make friends with a doxie?

Families that own dachshunds will tell you they love their pets. Their pets likely love them, too!

Dachshund History

The dachshund, or badger dog, is a long-bodied and short-legged dog. Dogs matching this **description** have been seen in historical accounts since the 1400s. As people began to **standardize** the breed in the 1600s, German hounds called *Deutsche Bracken* were crossbred with a terrier-type dog. This mix made the dachshund we know today.

Here Jane Baxter, a well-known actress from the 1930s, holds her pet dachshund in 1933.

Dachshunds became part of the American Kennel Club in 1885. By 1913, the dachshund was among the top 10 dog breeds in America. Dachshunds dropped out of this list during the beginning of **World War I**. They worked their way back into the list of the top 10 breeds by 1940, though.

Dachshunds became well-liked family pets in America in the 1900s. This dachshund says hello to a young family member in 1945.

Look, a Dachshund!

It is easy to spot a dachshund. These are short dogs, but they are quite long. Their legs and paws are very strong. These small dogs were first bred to dig. Their size and shape let them chase badgers right into their holes. Their long noses help them in their job as hunters, too. They are bred to be

Dachshunds were bred to be independent, or able to work well on their own. They were hunting in places where their owners could not help them!

fearless, too, so they can fight a badger to the death if needed.

Dachshunds come in two sizes, standard and miniature. Miniatures weigh up to 11 pounds (5 kg) and standard-size dogs weigh up to 32 pounds (14.5 kg). In either size, their teeth are sharp and strong.

These Doxies Look Different

In each size, there are three types of dachshund breeds, which are defined by their fur. These types are the smooth, wirehaired, and long-haired dachshunds.

The smooth dachshund has a short, shiny coat. Wirehaired dachshunds have short, thick outer coats and fine, very soft hairs in their undercoats. Long-haired dachshunds

This is a dachshund with a wirehaired coat.

This smooth-coated doxie has a beautiful dappled pattern on its fur.

have wavy hair on their ears, tail, feet, and body. Dachshunds can have fur that is one color, such as red, black, or tan. Dachshunds also are seen with two colors, often with tan as the second color. Dachshunds may also have dappled or brindle patterns on their fur.

Do you see the long, soft fur on this long-haired dachshund's ears?

A Friendly Companion

Dachshunds are playful and **loyal** pets. They become quite attached to their owners and want to be part of whatever their people are doing.

Doxies can also be **stubborn** and this can make them harder to train than some other breeds. However, being **consistent** with your dachshund will help

Puppies, including dachshund puppies, sometimes chew on things. Be sure to give your pet toys it can chew and then teach it to leave your belongings alone!

bring out the best of its **temperament**. Above all, treat your dachshund with love and respect. After all, the thing your dachshund wants most is to make you happy! This is what makes dachshunds such great family pets.

Dachshunds love their owners, including the children in their family.

Take Care of Your Dachshund

People who own dachshunds want them to be part of their families for a long time! You can help your dachshund live a long and happy life by taking good care of it. Every dachshund needs clean water and healthy food. Dachshund puppies nurse from their mothers for the first six weeks and then move on to dog food.

Dachshunds need plenty of exercise. Walking your pet can be a nice thing to do as a family!

Dachshunds are energetic dogs and enjoy getting out to play or walk. They once enjoyed chasing badgers into their holes. Today they love to chase birds, squirrels, and tennis balls. Doxies are always ready for play. Your pet will also need to be bathed sometimes, and it will need to visit the veterinarian at least once each year.

A veterinarian gives this dachshund a checkup. A yearly checkup lets you know if there are any changes to your pet's health.

Training Your Dachshund

Dachshund owners should train their dogs to let their natural good temperaments shine through. The dachshund can be a friendly dog that is good with children. This takes early **socialization** and consistent training, though. Your dachshund puppy should start meeting other people and dogs at

Teaching a dachshund to walk nicely on a leash will make walks more fun for the dog and its owner.

8 to 16 weeks. This will help it become comfortable and calm around others.

Your pet is counting on you to tell it what it should and should not do. Teach your dog to sit, stay, and come when you call. Training your dog can be a rewarding and fun time for both of you. It takes lots of patience, though.

This dachshund is learning how to shake, or give its paw to its owner. This can be a helpful skill to teach since you will need to cut your dog's nails every so often.

Keeping Busy

As you know, dachshunds were bred as hunting dogs. Some people still count on the dachshund's sharp sense of smell, its bravery, and its small size to hunt small animals. Most dachshunds today are found in homes, working as loving family pets!

Your dachshund likely enjoys challenges. You might take it to events

Dachshunds were bred for digging. Do not be surprised if your pet digs holes in your garden or sandbox if given the chance.

Dachshunds like to chase things, such as tennis balls. Playing catch can be a rewarding and fun game for you and your pet.

called Earthdog trials, or tests. In these events the dogs follow the scent of **prey** into tunnels. It is a great way for a dachshund to use its natural skills! Obedience, agility, field, and tracking trials all test their wits, too. Even playing fetch with a Frisbee puts your dachshund to work!

Look at this doxie go! Dachshunds love to run and play, which is why they make fun pets!

Why Pick a Doxie?

The dachshund has been well-liked for hundreds of years. Doxies have playful, sometimes funny personalities. Dachshunds are also known for being smart and independent. They like to be busy and to play games with you.

Do not pick a dachshund if you will have to leave it alone often. This is a dog that wants to be around people. It is curious and can get into trouble if left on its own too much. Taking good care of your doxie means you will have a loving friend for a long time to come!

Is a dachshund right for your family? It was for this one!

Dachshund Facts

1. Dachshunds are part of the hound group but have many similarities to the terrier breeds of dogs, too.

2. Dachshundlike dogs appear in artwork from ancient Egypt.

3. Dachshunds like to eat, so owners have to work hard to keep their pets at healthy weights.

4. Famous cartoon dachshunds include Itchy Itchiford from *All Dogs Go to Heaven* and Slinky from the *Toy Story* movies.

5. Brutus, a miniature dachshund, is the only Humane Society and veterinarian-approved skydiving animal!

6. Queen Victoria, painters Pablo Picasso and Andy Warhol, and President Grover Cleveland all owned dachshunds.

Glossary

breed (BREED) A group of animals that look alike and have the same relatives.

charm (CHAHRM) Ease at winning people's hearts.

consistent (kun-SIS-tent) Done the same way every time.

description (dih-SKRIP-shun) Words that give a picture.

domestic (duh-MES-tik) Relating to or used within a household.

loyal (LOY-ul) Faithful to a person or an idea.

obedience (oh-BEE-dee-ens) Being ready to do what you are told to do.

personality (per-sun-A-lih-tee) How a person or an animal acts with others.

prey (PRAY) An animal that is hunted by another animal for food.

social (SOH-shul) Living together in a group.

socialization (soh-shuh-luh-ZAY-shun) Learning to be friendly.

standardize (STAN-der-dyz) To make like others in a group.

stubborn (STUH-burn) Wanting to have one's own way.

temperament (TEM-pur-ment) Character, nature.

World War I (WURLD WOR WUN) The war fought between the Allies, which included Russia, France, Britain, Italy, the United States, Japan, and other countries, and the Central powers of Germany, Austria-Hungary, Turkey, and Bulgaria, from 1914 to 1918.

Index

Web Sites

Due to the changing nature of Internet links, PowerKids Press has developed an online list of Web sites related to the subject of this book. This site is updated regularly. Please use this link to access the list:
www.powerkidslinks.com/topd/dachs/